WALKER:
PUT A SOCK IN IT

by Tom Walker

DORRANCE
PUBLISHING CO
EST. 1920
PITTSBURGH, PENNSYLVANIA 15238

Dorrance Publishing Co
585 Alpha Drive
Suite 103
Pittsburgh, PA 15238

Visit our website at *www.dorrancebookstore.com*

ISBN: 978-1-4809-5589-9
eISBN: 978-1-4809-5566-0

CHAPTER ONE
THE EARLY YEARS

I was born in Milford, Utah on October 25, 1944, right in the middle of World War II. I remember as a youth having food shortages due to the war and eating things that I would never touch as an adult. I remember sitting at the kitchen table until midnight in front of a bowl of lima beans. I wasn't about to eat them, and Mom wasn't about to let them go to waste. We finally negotiated a treaty, and I had one more spoonful of the nasty legumes and was allowed to go to bed. This scene was repeated several times when stewed tomatoes, hominy, or spinach was served. One day, I thought I was pretty clever when I ate all of the ice cream in the carton, filled the container with water, and put it back in the freezer. Mom knew exactly who the culprit was, and I got a well deserved timeout. That's how I got the nickname Homgry, because I was always hungry. I became the scape-goat because my brothers and sisters knew I would fall for anything. They would send me to Dad and have me ask for something they wanted. I would ask Dad, and he would tell me no. I would return to my siblings and they would beat me up for not being convincing enough and send me back again to negotiate. Dad would spank me and send me away. Such was the life of the fourth child. One time, they strapped me on a tree sapling and bent it over and let it go. I was launched about fifty feet in the air and had a less-than-successful landing. An-other time, after watching a Western movie, I was tied to a post in the middle of an ant bed. Mom rescued me just in time to save me from being eaten by red ants. Things got worse from that time forward. I became the model when my oldest sister decided to be a barber. That experience ended with a severe cut on my right ear. A baseball game on the front lawn ended with me getting stitches in my right eyebrow, having been hit by the bat. It's a wonder I survived.

All four of us slept in the same bed. We would tickle backs until we got tired enough to go to sleep. Of course, we made a lot of noise, and Dad would threaten us that the next time he had to call out, he would bring a belt. We heard him coming, and everyone reached for covers. Everyone got some but me, and I got the belt as they were protected by the blankets.

One Saturday, the family was gone to town, and Brother Dick and I were left at home to do chores. We rented an old farmhouse about ten miles from town, and Saturdays were spent doing chores. We thought we saw a prowler in the corral, and we became frightened. We quickly loaded the shotgun and were ready for an intruder. Brother Dick was walking across the living room with shotgun in hand when Skeeter, our family dog, went dashing across the floor. Dick turned suddenly to see what was happening and hit the butt of the shotgun on the stove, causing the gun to go off. Luckily, he shot a hole in the floor. We quickly assessed the damages and pulled an area rug over the hole in the floor. Then we left the house to go to a neighbor's house to play. When the family came home, they could smell the gunpowder, and they saw the rug in an unusual place. Of course my parents were worried, not knowing what had happened. When we came home in a few hours, we got grounded for life.

My father, Marion Henry Walker, was born and raised in Western Kentucky, the son of a sharecropper coal miner. His parents were Glover and Nonie Walker, who were raised in near poverty conditions. Glover was and orphan who was raised by a muleskinner after his father died drowning in a ditch in a drunken stupor. Glover ran away at the age of seventeen to make it on his own. He met Nonie and they became fast friends. She was only fifteen and came from a large family of seven girls and one boy. They'd not been friends very long when they decided to get married. They were too young to marry in Kentucky, so they went across the state line into Indiana where they could marry without that restriction. I think they lied about their age anyway, just for insurance. My dad was born before Nonie turned sixteen.

My Mother, Janet Rollins, was born and raised near Minersville, Utah, a farming community of about 500 people. She was a good student and loved to read and recite poetry. She met my dad as he was stationed in nearby Milford working with the CCCs (Civilian Conservation Corps). They married and moved to Southern California, still with the CCC. Eventually, they moved back to Milford, where Dad hired on with the Union Pacific Railroad as a brakeman. We lived in Milford most of my growing up years. Dad was a sports fanatic and fol-

Area Games. Coaches Jean Moore (L) and Tom Walker ® start the recent Cedar City Special Olympics.

Area Games

Every year in May, we would attend the state games held in Salt Lake or Provo. It was always the highlight of the year for the students, and for me as well. We spent all year fundraising in order to make the trip. We sold popcorn during the lunchtime for months in advance. We had our own commercial popcorn popper and were able to make $20 to $30 dollars a day selling popcorn through the outside window of our classroom to students and teachers at the school.

One year, the games were held at the University of Utah in Salt Lake City. We were lined up on the track ready for the opening ceremonies and the parade of athletes. All of the teams were decked out in team uniforms, carrying flags and waving banners. It was very exciting. Then I looked around and felt very strange. All of a sudden, I realized I was in the minority, as everywhere I looked was the face of a person with disabilities. That was the day I understood how they must feel living in a world with people who didn't know or understand what they were going through because of their disability. It gave me an entirely different perspective into the importance of what I was doing.

That day, there were several people who caught my attention. One was a nice looking young man who appeared to be in his mid-twenties. I wasn't sure if he was a coach or an athlete. I kept watching him with interest. Finally, when he stood on his head on the grass, I figured it out.

Another young man also caught my eye, and I was puzzled with the same question. Finally, I decided to ask him a question. I asked him the question, and when he answered me with some language that was unintelligible, I had my answer. After that, I tried not to judge people by first impression and to take them for who they were.

The State Games were always very exciting and very well organized. The organizers not only planned the games themselves, but also other activities such as dances, alternate activities, and arranged for host families for our students with whom they would spend the night. It was always a worry sending our students off with strangers. We worried that they wouldn't behave well, or that they'd be afraid of their new hosts. We always gave the hosts a phone number where we could be reached.

One year, the games were being held in Provo and hosted by Brigham Young University. When we arrived at the games, we were given some college students to assist us with the student athletes. We assigned two young women to be with Tammy, a teenage girl with autism. They took her and everything seemed to be fine. About fifteen minutes later, one of the girls returned, holding Tammy's tee shirt. She told me that Tammy ran away and was stripping as she ran. I hurried to try and find Tammy, knowing that she would be out of control. She'd done this at school on occasion when she became frustrated. I followed along, picking up articles of clothing as I went. Soon I came to the busy University Avenue where there was a crossing guard at the intersection. I asked him if he'd seen a naked girl running down the street. He said, "No. How old is she, and what does she look like?" I proceeded down the street and continued to follow the trail of clothing. Finally, I found her in an apartment complex playground playing on a rocking horse. She was completely naked and having a great time. As I approached her, she started to run. I quickly caught her, took off my tee shirt, and put it on her. Then I had the dubious task of getting her back to the bus. In the meantime, the university students had gathered up Tammy's clothing and were looking for me. We didn't meet up with them, and I was looking pretty stupid and embarrassed walking down the street with a half-naked girl and me in my underwear from the waist up.

That same year, we had another younger girl whose name was Tammy also; we called her little Tammy. She was a seven-year-old with Down syndrome. She was also a runner and got away from her host. We looked everywhere for her and finally went to the security station to see if she'd been spotted. The student at the station got on her walkie-talkie and asked the others if they'd seen little Tammy. When the reply came back, it was another student who said, "Yes, I have little Tammy with me; I can remember her from last year when she ran away then." How embarrassing is it to lose the same girl two years in a row and to be rescued for a second time by the same volunteer?

Naomi, the same girl who said, "Who died and made you boss?" came up missing when she wandered off from her host student. We looked for her for hours and had everyone trying to find her. We finally found her asleep on the bus when one of the aides went to the bus to get something.

On our way home that year, one of the older girls was having a problem and was having her period. We stopped at a service station so the women could help her. They went into the restroom. Soon one of them came back and asked me for some change because they needed to buy a tampon. A little girl overheard the conversation and yelled at the top of her lungs, "Pom poms; I love them. I want some too."

We became involved in the run, dribble, and shoot competition that became an annual event and was usually hosted by the University of Utah in Salt Lake City. One year, I took three teenage boys to the competition. We left Cedar City in the early afternoon headed for Salt Lake. Soon after our departure, Emery reached over the seat from the back and said, "Aakow, (that what he called me because he couldn't say Walker), "Aaburda, enchfies, Coke." Interpreted, that meant hamburger, French fries, and a Coke. I told him he'd have to wait because it wasn't time to eat yet, and besides, we were miles from any fast food restaurants. About every twenty minutes, he would reach over the seat and grab my shoulder and give me the same pleading request. By the time we got to Provo, he was up to 5 hamburgers. We pulled in at a McDonald's Restaurant. I left one adult in the car with the other boys and took Emery with me to order the food. As soon as we entered the front door, Emery yelled, "Ah ha," as he rushed the to counter. The place was very busy, and suddenly it became deathly silent. The cashier came running and asked if she could help. Emery said, "Five aaburdas, enchfies, Coke." I translated for the cashier and ordered for everyone. When the food was ready, I told Emery to take the food to the car while I paid the bill. When I came outside, there he was headed for the wrong car. An older woman inside the car saw him coming and locked all the doors. Emery tried to get in and became frustrated, thinking that the other students were playing with him. He put the bags of food on the ground and started to rock the car. The woman inside the car was bouncing all over with a terrified scream and panicked look on her face. All I could do was laugh, it was so funny. Finally, I ran over and told Emery he was at the wrong car. The woman in the car started the engine and ripped out of there, flipping us off as she drove. I've always loved McDonald's since that day.

Emery lived across the street from one of the local elementary schools. He loved to go there after school and play on the grounds. He would terrorize the small children because of his size and demeanor. One day, he was hiding in the school when an Oriental woman was walking down the hall. He jumped out and grabbed her and hugged her with all his might. She broke away and ran screaming down the hall, yelling, "Giant!" When Emery would capture someone, he would just lie on top of them and laugh. I spent a great deal of time rescuing Emery's victims. Emery was the source of some great adventures. One day, he was chasing a student down the hall when he ran into the door with a crash bar. He shattered the glass in the door and was hanging over the bar when I rescued him. It took a few stitches and lots of Band Aids to patch him up. He was more careful about running into doors after that.

My wife and I on occasion would travel south about fifty miles to the Boilers, a mineral hot springs resort. We invited Emery to go with us one night. He had a great time and so did we, except when he tried to make out with my wife. My wife insisted we not invite him again.

Chapter 5
International Games

Brockport, New York

Every four years, Special Olympics International Games is held at a university site. The schools bid for the games much the same as the World Olympics. Special Olympics was founded in 1968 by Eunice Kennedy Shriver. The first international games were held at Soldiers Field in Chicago. Since that time, the Special Olympics International Games have been held every four years at a university site.

Each state as well as representatives from foreign nations have the opportunity of selecting a team of thirty-six Special Olympians to represent their state or country. The motto of the Special Olympics is, "Let me win. But if I cannot win, let me be brave in the attempt." This credo has inspired thousands of communities and organizations and millions of special athletes to participate in Special Olympics and has changed their lives for the better.

I had the opportunity to attend two International Special Olympic Games. The first one was held in upstate New York in Brockport. Thirty-six athletes and twelve coaches attended the games. We all met in Salt Lake City where we were given our travel uniforms and instructions regarding the trip to Brockport. We all stayed at the Olympus Hotel in Salt Lake City, where we had an opportunity to meet the other coaches and athletes. Matching pullover windbreakers were issued so we could keep track of everyone. The coaches wore windbreakers with a navy blue body and white sleeves. The athletes wore just the opposite: white body with blue sleeves. We boarded the plane in Salt Lake and traveled to Chicago, where we changed planes. When we boarded the plane, we were announced as the Special Olympics team from Utah. We got loud cheers and warm greetings. The flight attendants were very helpful to get us settled. When the plane took off, all of our athletes yelled and cheered. They loved the little buttons above the seats, and especially the one that had the shape of a woman. They kept the attendant running the entire flight. One of the boys sitting by me kept pressing the button and asking for Coke. Finally, after five Cokes, the attendant said, "That's five; don't you need to go to the restroom?" When we got off the plane, the attendants looked worn out, their hair a mess and blouses hanging over their skirts. I'm sure they were anxious to kiss us goodbye.

While waiting in Chicago for our next flight, I kept watching one of the athletes. He seemed pretty normal to me, but I wasn't sure after previous experiences in Provo and Salt Lake. I walked over to him and started to talk with him, and I was even more confused. He had the same windbreaker as all of the athletes. Finally, I asked him some leading questions, and he told me he was a coach from Northern Utah. He said they were out of coaches' windbreakers in his size, so he got one of the athlete's uniforms. He said he was sick of being treated as if he were retarded. We both had a good laugh.

On the next flight, we headed for Rochester, New York. We had a similar experience with the flight attendant as on the first leg of our journey, but it was a shorter flight, so Alan drank only four Cokes. When we arrived in Rochester, we were greeted by hosts from Brockport and ushered to a waiting school bus and were shuttled to the campus of Brockport College. We were taken to dormitories and we got settled. We were there for five days and were treated like royalty.

The day after we arrived, we were taken by bus to Lake Ontario, where residents were waiting to take us sailing on the lake in their magnificent sailboats. After sailing for about an hour, we went walking along the shoreline. People who owned homes along the shore were there to welcome us and invite us in for refreshments. Several times we were invited in for cookies, cakes, and beverages.

The next day, the games began. It was amazing because that small college didn't have a football stadium on campus. The International Special Olympics built a stadium for the college in appreciation for hosting the games on their campus. Our athletes did a wonderful job and represented us well. They earned many medals, but most of all had a great time.

The day before the games ended, we were loaded on 200 school buses and transported to Buffalo, New York, where we went to the Niagara Falls. The buses were organized in waves of fifty each, with a medical bus for each wave and an empty bus just in case one broke down. At one point, when we neared Buffalo, they stopped all traffic and took us on a detour from one freeway to another to save time and expedite our travel. The athletes were totally amazed at the sight of the falls and the power of the water rushing down the steep cliff.

After looking at the falls, we went to an adjacent park where volunteers served a wonderful barbecue. There were more than two thousand athletes and coaches who were fed and entertained by senior citizen volunteers who loved every minute of it. That was a great day.

The games at Brockport were truly amazing. Every day, people came though the dorms and gave us gifts. They gave us cameras, belts, tee shirts, bandanas, and other gifts. The food was great and the volunteers were outstanding

Baton Rouge, Louisiana

Prior to leaving for the next Olympics, I had an assignment to help set up tents at the area girls' camp for our church. One of the local Special Olympians was to accompany me to the games, and I thought I would take him with me to help set up tents the day before we left. We drove up the mountain to the girls' camp and spent several hours getting camp ready. While we were there, it started to rain. It rained hard for over an hour. When we tried to leave girls' camp, the truck got stuck in the mud, and the more we tried to get out, the worse it got. That area known as Webster's Flat is mostly clay, and very slippery when it gets wet. We had to make a five-mile-walk until we were able to catch a ride off the mountain to get home. Alan was so mad at me, and he kept saying, "Walker, I'm going to kill you," over and over again as he slipped all over the road in his brand new cowboy boots that were totally covered in mud.

My next experience with International Special Olympics was four years after Brockport when the games were hosted at Louisiana State University in Baton Rouge, La. Again, there were thirty-six athletes and twelve couches. We flew directly from Salt Lake City to Baton Rouge, and again were greeted by volunteers and bussed to the university dormitories.

Opening Ceremony. July 12, 1983. Tiger Stadium LSU

The International Special Olympics donated and built a new aquatic center on the campus of LSU in return for hosting the games. It was the middle of the summer and it was extremely hot and humid. I can remember drinking liquids all day long and never once having to use the restroom because I was dripping wet from perspiration.

Opening ceremonies were held at Tiger Stadium on the campus of LSU. The state delegations lined up alphabetically, with foreign nation delegations following. As we came out of the tunnel to the field, it was breathtaking. There were thousands of people in the stadium cheering and waving as the national anthem was played on the sound system. We felt like heroes being welcomed home from battle. The opening ceremonies were spectacular.

Most of our athletes participated in track and field rather than the other events, so we spent most of our time there. A few of our athletes participated in gymnastics and played team basketball.

I will never forget a black runner who had no legs. When I saw him lined up for the race, I thought he'd be totally embarrassed as the others ran off and left him. The starting gun sounded and the race began. This young runner was amazing. He'd become so proficient with his crutches that he moved as quickly as the others. He would reach out with his crutches and swing his body through with great speed and grace. He did this over and over again and came to the finish line well ahead of the other athletes. The spectators went wild at the sight of this brave young runner and his courage. Hugs and kisses abounded on both the field and on the track. That day, this runner earned more than a gold medal; he earned the love and respect of everyone who witnessed the event.

One day at the track, I was watching with great anticipation as one of our athletes was lined up for the 400-meter run. The race began and they were pretty evenly matched. Things were nip and tuck and the runners were coming around the last turn for the finish line. All of a sudden, one of the runners stumbled and fell to the track. The other runners stopped one by one and came back to help the fallen runner. Then in unison, all of the runners, arm in arm, crossed the finish line together. That day everyone was a winner. The Special Olympics Oath ran through my mind: "Let me win, but if I cannot win, let me be brave in the attempt." All of the runners were brave in the attempt. Friendship and bravery was much more important to those runners than a gold or silver or bronze medal. And that was the theme of this International Games for me. I saw brave young athletes fall from the parallel bars, get up, and continue, aided by others. I saw swimmers lifted from the pool after a race when their energy was all spent and they couldn't stand. I saw athletes wrapping the ankles of their friends who'd fallen in the standing long jump and were injured. I saw basketball teams work together to play other teams where the excitement of the game was more important than the outcome or the final score. Yes, we could all learn a lesson from those brave Special Olympians.

Everyone ate their meals a central cafeteria on campus. One evening, I was one of the last to go through the cafeteria line and finish eating. The dinner was prepared, served, and hosted by senior citizen volunteers. They were very hospitable and friendly to everyone. When I finished eating, I took my tray to the dish room so it could be washed. There was a large tub for the silverware. I threw my silverware in the tub. An older volunteer was watching me and said, "Good shot, do you throw the softball in the games?" I knew that he thought I was one of the athletes. I didn't want to embarrass him, so I shook my head and said, "Ya, ya," in my best retarded voice. I cracked up all the way to the dormitory.

Several celebrities were present at those games; Rafer Johnson and Mohammad Ali, just to name a few. Eunice Kennedy Shriver was the keynote speaker at the opening ceremonies.

The last night of the games was highlighted by a dance of the athletes. It was a grand affair with many young people from the community attending. One of our athletes was in a wheelchair and was totally excited about the dance. When we got to the dance, she was worried that everyone would stare at her. Not long after we arrived, I took her to the dance floor and we danced around to the music, doing wheelies in her wheelchair. The media was there covering the event, and she became the bell of the ball, being captured by the TV cameras. After that, everyone wanted to dance with her and try new tricks with the wheelchair. I'm sure that night was the highlight of the games for her, and maybe the best night of her life.

Like all good things, this International Games came to an end. I took with me some new friends, the experience of eating craw daddies, the memories of brave and courageous athletes, and the spirit of the great volunteers I met on the campus of LSU.

CHAPTER 6
DISNEYLAND

One year, as school began, we used some Disney films as part of the curriculum, and we learned some familiar songs that came from the films. I remember that the song "Hi ho, hi ho, it's off to work we go—," was one of the favorites from the movie "Snow White and the Seven Dwarfs." John David especially liked "Grumpy" in the movie. He would mimic the movie by saying, "You must be Grumpy." As we explored the world of Disney further, we asked the students if they'd ever been to Disneyland. None of them had ever been there, so we thought it would be fun to investigate the possibility of going there with our students. We inquired with the school district about the trip, and we were given permission as long as there was no expense incurred by the district.

How would we raise the money necessary to fund transportation, lodging, entrance to Disneyland, and meals? We knew the parents would help but wouldn't be able to finance the entire adventure. After some time of considering different options, we decided we'd sell popcorn during the lunch period every day until we earned enough to fund the trip. We'd sold popcorn in the past to help with our Special Olympics trips and knew the teachers and students at the school would support us. We also had the support of the local ARC (Association of Retarded Citizens). The ARC Board of Directors also pledged some money for the activity as long as some of the older citizens with disabilities were involved. So with the approval and blessing of everyone needed, we became popcorn vendors. We had a commercial popcorn popper and a resource to buy materials, so we were ready to go.

We averaged about $50.00 a day in popcorn sales, and at twenty-five cents a bag, that was a lot of popcorn being sold out the window of our classroom each day. Of course, many times students would hand us a dollar and say, "keep the change." We needed to raise about $600.00 in addition to the funding from the ARC, so within a month we were able to raise enough to finance the trip. Since I had a commercial driver's license with a certificate to drive a school bus, I became the designated driver. We planned on using a Mini Bus carrying eighteen passengers, which worked out just right to carry twelve students, a driver, classroom aides, and several parents.

For two weeks prior to the trip we made cookies, candy, and other treats to take on the trip. Because the treats were so good, we had to make them several times, because the school kids kept finding our hiding place and eating the goodies. We were able to secure lodging directly across the street from Disneyland at a discounted rate because or our unique situation. We also received special group discounts at Disneyland and Universal Studios. Soon the travel plans were finalized and the dates were set.

Several parents were invited to accompany us to help with the special needs of our students. Without the parents, we wouldn't have been able to make the trip. Of course we had many offers from faculty members and students from the school to go along with us to help, but we were limited by the size of the school bus. We did take Rob, a college student who was doing a practicum with us. He was a big help.

Arriving in Las Vegas, we needed a lunch and restroom break. Finding a neighborhood park, we stopped for lunch. Sack lunches had been prepared by the school lunch ladies. We spread out on the lawn eating our lunch, when we noticed one of the mothers going door to door across the street. Looking at each other, we wondering what she was doing. As it turns out, there were no restrooms in the park, and the mother was trying to find a neighbor who would let her use their restroom.

Later, as we were driving along I-15, I asked one of the classroom aides to break out some of the cookies we'd made for the trip. She went to the back of the bus and came back to tell me that everything was gone. The same mother who'd gone door to door looking for a restroom had eaten all of our goodies. The only thing left was the empty containers and a few crumbs. She was also the same mother who tried to use food stamps in the fast food places we visited. She also kept all of the plastic ware and paper plates and cups we used at fast food places. She took them home to reuse and was so excited that she wouldn't have to wash dishes for a month.

We arrived in Anaheim in the early evening and got settled in our motel rooms. We had three students to one adult in every room. Most of our meals were eaten at a Sambo's restaurant near the motel. When we went for dinner at the restaurant, the hostess came running with a painful look on her face. I told her there were seventeen of us and she immediately called for the manager. We were escorted to the very back of the restaurant to a private room where we wouldn't gross out any of the other diners.

The same routine was repeated every time we visited the restaurant. It was especially funny when we went for breakfast, because Emery was famished. As we were walking to the back of the restaurant, he picked up several pancakes and slices of toast from the plates of patrons. They were mortified of course, and I had some great explaining to do. No wonder we had our own private dining room.

The next day, we went to Disneyland, and what an experience it was. The kids had a great time. We received some wonderful looks from everyone as we shuffled from one attraction to the other. Emery of course pooped out on us early, so we rented a wheelchair for him. It was fun to push him around and watch the looks on people's faces when he jumped out of the wheelchair and ran to the front of the line. We rode the "It's a Small World" attraction so many times that the attendants knew us by our first names.

At about mid-afternoon, we sat down on a bench to take a rest. It just so happened that a large group of about 200 students with disabilities from Washington State was in the park that day. I was sitting next to Tammi, a thirteen-year-old girl with Down syndrome. As the group from Washington walked by, she kept turning her head back and forth as they passed us by. When they were all by us, she looked at me and said, "Walker, who were all the weirdoes?" So how do you respond to that question? I merely said, "Well, that's the pot calling the kettle black." She just looked at me and smiled.

The next day, we went to Universal Studios for another adventure. This time, we split up in small groups of five or six, because everyone had different interests. We had a great day and things went well until we gathered to exit the park. The same mother who ate all of the goodies was nowhere to be found. We looked all over for her and even had her paged. Finally, she came huffing up, loaded for bear. When I inquired as to her whereabouts, she informed me that she was waiting for her screen test. When I told her we had to leave, she fell to the ground and threw a royal fit right there in front of everyone. If you haven't figured it out yet, she wasn't playing with a full deck. I guess this is as good a time as any to relate another of her stories.

One day, her son Scott was having a tough time at school. He was picking imaginary bugs out of the air and crying as he did so. I called his mother, Mrs. "C," and related to her what Scott was doing. She told me she would come and take him home. When she arrived, she went to Scott and patted him on the head and said, "It's okay, Scott, I'll take you home and give you an enema." I didn't go there; I didn't want to know. I just waved goodbye as they walked out the door, scratching my head.

Anyway, we finally got Mrs. "C" back on the bus and headed back to the motel. Someone mentioned that we were near the famous farmer's market and should go. I made an illegal U-turn and drove to the farmer's market. Our kids squeezed all the tomatoes, oranges, and grapes, manhandled the lettuce and other produce, and we were finally asked to "get the hell out." Pretty rude, don't you think?

So off we went back to the motel for another trip to Sambo's restaurant. This time, when we were greeted by the hostess, she said, "The rest of your group is in the back." You guessed it; we joined the group from Washington. Now Tammi was totally frustrated, looked at me, and said, "Not again!"

Before we left California, we went to Long Beach where my Aunt Glenna lived. She agreed to have us come to visit and she would feed us a snack. She really didn't know what she was volunteering for. Most of the time we were there, she stood with her mouth open, whispering things like, "Oh my—, and "Unbelievable," and "Are you kidding?" She was very gracious, and when we left, she said, "It was good to have you, but next time, I'll plan to be out of town."

We left a lasting impression on Southern California and especially that little hostess at Sambo's restaurant. We left the next morning for our trip home. We only had three potty breaks along the way, and we stopped in Las Vegas at McDonald's for lunch. This time, it was Jeffrey, who was the main attraction, not Emery. Jeff went directly to the play place where a little boy of about five or six was sitting eating his lunch. Jeff made some weird noises that only he could make and frightened the boy, who immediately went running. Then Jeff sat down and ate the little boy's lunch. His mother soon came and gave me a scotch blessing. By now I was getting used to it.

Not long after we left Las Vegas, we were cruising down the freeway, and things were going well. Alan was fast asleep, which was a good thing. We were passing a diesel truck that was towing another diesel truck cab. Alan woke up and looked out the window. He saw the diesel truck cab facing our bus and thought it was coming right at us. He jumped out of his seat screaming and ran for the wheel of the bus. We nearly had a fatal accident, but one of the aides pulled him back to his seat.

We had so much fun on that trip that we planned another trip the next year, but this time we invited other special ed classes to join us, and we took a big bus with a professional bus driver at the wheel. It was a pretty average trip, and nothing out of the ordinary happened, except for the time we sideswiped that car in the parking lot at Sea World.

CHAPTER 7
INCLUSION

Sara was walking down the hall with one of the school aides when Janet from the state office of education stopped her and leaned down to say something to her. Immediately, Sara said, "Get out of my face." This is the same Sara who never spoke anything independently before inclusion. She always repeated words others spoke to her, prior to implementing inclusion in the school district.

During the late eighties, there was a nationwide movement to include students with disabilities in the regular classroom setting along with their non-disabled peers. The thought of having a disabled student in the regular classroom stirred panic in the minds of the majority of teachers on all levels of education and in every discipline. A task force was initiated to help with the transition. The local school district committee consisted of several special educators—elementary, intermediate, and secondary teachers. Monthly training was offered by the state of Utah to help with the transition. My entire career had been in the self-contained classroom with twelve to fourteen students. Now I had the great opportunity to assimilate my students in the regular classroom in their neighborhood schools. The task seemed daunting, and we were all frightened. When school started that year, every teacher with one of my kids wanted me in the classroom all of the time, and every time I came to check on them, the teacher wanted me to stay. My students were frightened, and they struggled in the regular classroom, away from the safety of the self-contained setting. At first, we all had our doubts as to if this would really work. We all struggled early on. It was hard for me to create IEPs (Individualized Education Plans) for my students when I wasn't there all the time to implement the curriculum and work on strategies to help them progress. After several weeks, things started to change for the better for all of us.

I recall going to visit Sara in the third grade one day at East Elementary School. One of her goals was stair climbing. We constructed as small set of portable steps for her to use in the classroom for practice. Sara's teacher informed me that the stairs were no longer needed, because Sara had mastered stair climbing. When I inquired as to how that happened, she took me to the playground. A classmate took Sara by the hand and went to the slide. She stood behind Sara and tapped her behind the knees as she climbed the stairs of the slide. Sara climbed the stairs as normal as any other child within a few weeks in a natural setting, and not one arranged by us to teach the skill. Inclusion was working, and Sara was being taught by her peers rather than her teacher or aide.

Later that school year, I went to visit Sara's mother to see how things were going at home. Her mom told me several stories about Sara being invited to birthday parties and sleepovers for the first time in her life. She also told me about a neighbor boy who built a snowman in Sara's front yard. He turned the face of the snowman toward the front window of Sara's home so she could see it better. She was now for the first time using language independently, and not repeating what she heard. One day, Sara took a glass from the kitchen cabinet and plunked it down on the table where her father was sitting and said, "Coke, damn it." Her father was so shocked at the outburst that he immediately poured her a Coke.

I found the same was true of all of my students. They were making amazing progress in the regular classroom, mostly because of the positive interaction between them and their classroom peers. I found that as the school year progressed, I was needed less and less, and the classroom teachers were finally treating them as one of their students and not referring to them as one of my students.

Stephanie, another student with Down syndrome attended the South Elementary School. She was in a regular fifth grade classroom. When she threw a fit in the classroom or on the playground, it was her classmates rather than her teacher who did the correction. When she exhibited bad behavior, her friends would tell her to "knock it off" and that they weren't going to play with her if she didn't change her behavior. Soon, Stephanie was behaving well in the regular education setting with the help of her peers. She's the same student who told me to "Put a thock in it" when we were in the self contained setting.

Two other students, Nate and Brent, were kindergarten students when we started to implement inclusion. Both students came from very supportive homes. Their parents were always very helpful and worked with their students at home to enhance their education at school. Both students went to kindergarten like any other student. They progressed well in that setting and were immediately accepted by their peers as "one of the guys." Some minor behavior modification was needed for both of them. Nate pulled the fire alarm several times and caused a minor panic in the school when he did it. That was a rewarding behavior for him, and it took some shaping to extinguish that behavior. Brent did pretty well, except when he refused to do something. He would be passive-aggressive and would politely refuse to do certain things because he was "too tired."

Two nine-year old boys were enrolled at the North Elementary School. They were good buddies and got along well. They were completely integrated in the regular classroom and did very well with some monitoring from a classroom aide. One day, I was following them down the hall and overheard their conversation. It was a few days after I'd been hired as the Principal of North Elementary School for the following school year. They were talking about me, and one of them said, "I think Walker will be a pretty good President." I walked proudly all that day.

Did inclusion really work? I believe it was something that should have happened many years before it did. Everyone benefitted from inclusion. Regular classroom peers became more understanding and tolerant because of inclusion. Teachers became better because they had to think outside the box and initiate classroom procedures that were geared to all students and not just those who learned at a normal rate. The phrase "All Means All" was adopted statewide in all schools and in all settings. Now, inclusion is practiced nationwide, and students with disabilities are enrolled in regular education classrooms as a matter of common practice, with few exceptions. Students with profound disabilities are sometimes served in a self-contained setting where they can be served better. I'm happy that I played a small part in helping to create inclusive practices in the Iron County School District.

THE END